Feedback
REVOLUTION

Building Relationships
& Boosting Results

Marjorie M. Mauldin

FILLMORE
PRESS

Feedback Revolution
Building Relationships
& Boosting Results

www.executiveforum.net

ISBN # 978-0-9982908-0-5

Published by Fillmore Press. Printed in the USA.

Cover by BASS Creative.

Composition by Barbara Alber

Feedback is information that is shared with a person or group for the distinct purpose of improving results or relationships. Effective feedback is not venting, blaming, shaming or yielding to excuses.

Table of Contents

Introduction

When Peter McLaughlin and I first began talking about the topics of communication and feedback specifically, we quickly realized we had several things in common. We both felt that we were not particularly effective in giving feedback. In fact, we felt that we were pretty bad.

We enjoyed the challenge and the positive results that come with a successful feedback conversation. We wondered why we had not naturally learned to give feedback. We agreed that if we were provided with a roadmap or model for giving feedback, we would have performed much more effectively in such situations. Looking back at particular examples, we both had a sense of delight from the positive encounters, and a sense of dread over the sessions that left us feeling discouraged, beaten down and lackluster.

So why did we begin a project filled with such negative emotion? The answer—both to improve our own feedback skills and to examine what it would take to teach a new perspective and help "turn the opinion tide" that has made feedback a dreaded negative topic.

Who doesn't want to get better? Have you ever known anyone who said, "Nah, I'll just stay mediocre and by the way, I don't want a raise, promotion or exciting project..." Probably not. Our internal drive propels us to strive, learn and improve.

We soon learned that we were not the only people to feel this way. Leaders, managers, employees, athletes, and students all want to perform at their highest level and they want the people they work with to be able to do the same.

Imagine you are in a competition and someone comes to you with 2-3 "secrets" that will give you an edge over the competition. You would be all ears—eager to listen and incorporate the "secrets" into your plan!

So why is it that when our boss comes to us with our Personal Improvement Plan (PIP) we dread the conversation, make up stories about how we are better than they think, and generally stress out about the whole situation? I would venture to say our bosses were not good at giving feedback either.

Most people (like me and Peter) toggle between the continuum of cheerleading (*"Good job," "Great progress," "Keep up the good work!"*) and criticism (*"You had 7 errors in the report," "Your style is abrasive," "Just do your job."*). Peter and I had not realized that there is a happy medium between the two, and we discovered that we were well-prepared to build out the specifics of that happy medium!

As we developed the best practice model and the skills associated with its 5 steps, we learned that there were two intertwined factors—competence and confidence. When you are competent in a particular skill set (giving feedback)—your competence drives confidence. When you are confident, your approach to a difficult discussion becomes filled with positive emotions, eagerness to dive in, and a flexible attitude to understand and coach—not to blame and shame.

With that realization, we tackled the project of developing not only a manuscript for *Feedback Revolution,* also a training program, *iLoveFeedback*®. Our work together was exciting, invigorating, challenging and an opportunity to practice the skills we hoped to teach.

With Peter, the Executive Forum team was able to research and better understand the role effective feedback plays in the life of both the organization and its employees. Sadly, Peter—our friend, colleague and mentor—passed away in 2014. He is greatly missed for his intellect, humor, charm and the energy he gave to all of us.

We carry the mantle of our work in Peter's memory and will be forever grateful to have had the opportunity to work, learn and have fun completing this project. Peter McLaughlin's legacy is one we are most proud to continue building upon.

Margie Mauldin

Acknowledgements

No book, I've discovered, is written in a vacuum. That certainly applies, as it should, to a book about Feedback!

The process of creating a book is an interesting one—and one that feels a little like, hurry up—now wait. When we hurried, our race was to capture an idea that seemingly came out of nowhere at just the right moment to perfectly illustrate a point. As we waited for the stories, tips, tools and tactics to gel, the process sometimes felt like it would take forever. Keith Ferrell, you were a very patient man when editing early versions of the manuscript and polishing sections as we completed them one by one. Our conference calls always brightened my day—even when my writing didn't!

Particular thanks to Beth Wolfson and Alana Berland who worked to help guide the development of the *iLoveFeedback*® model and training program.

To Karyn Guilford, one of the most skilled business professionals I have ever worked with and who demonstrates the skills in a natural and easy way, my deep appreciation.

Michele Demark, Karyn Ruth White and Debra Fine, thank you for your coaching and support.

Bob and AmyBeth Stewart at BASS Creative worked their magic to create the look and feel of the completed manuscript and cover design.

Special thanks to my family. Mom, Dad who loved and supported me and challenged me to do my best. My sisters, Trixie and Martha, successful entrepreneurs, wonderful women, and my best friends.

Finally, my thanks to our children Abby and Will, who provided a lab for social and behavioral experimentation when you were teenagers, and who have become wonderful, talented and hardworking adults.

And my husband, Manning, thank you for providing stability and support for the roller coaster ride of a small business. Knowing you were there made all the difference!

Love to you all,

Margie

ONE

The Feedback Revolution Has Arrived—Just in Time!

The annual performance review is dead! Long live—

Feedback!

But not the feedback we used to know.

Over the past few years, the flurry of companies announcing their abandonment of formal performance reviews and evaluations has become a blizzard. Companies as large and long-lived as GE are eliminating form-driven performance evaluations and their generally perfunctory, ratings-scale approach to evaluation and, more critically, essential communication between managers and direct reports. Organizations and institutions of all sizes are following suit.

While it's still a bit premature to proclaim the annual by-the-numbers performance review to be, like the Wicked Witch of the East, "really most sincerely dead," there's little doubt that the ritual—and it was a ritual, dreaded by both reviewer and recipient, manager and managed, and rarely effective for either—is rapidly becoming a thing of the past.

A relic.

A fossil.

A memory—and not a fond one.

Few management tools and processes were as well-established—and entrenched—as the performance review, yet even fewer were more disliked. Hated would not be too strong a word for the feelings of most managers and employees toward performance evaluations.

The Society for Human Resource Management, in fact, found in 2015 that 95% of survey recipients were unhappy with their employer's approach to evaluating performance. A study from CEB found that 65% of employees felt that the performance review process harmed rather than helped improve their productivity.

I could offer more statistics, but if your work experience has been like mine, I don't need to. Whichever side of the desk we've found ourselves on when the performance review date arrives, we've all experienced the anxiety, trepidation and the irritation that accompanies seeing our year's work reduced to a programmatic set of check-boxes and number-codes on an impersonal form. Or, when in management, having to reduce a year of our direct reports' efforts to a series of tick-marks and numerals.

So good riddance to the ritual!

But what I find missing in most of the press commentary on the performance review's terminal condition is enlightened and thoughtful consideration of what will take its place.

There's talk of replacing the performance review with specialized apps, with more frequent formal "performance conversations," with other processes and tools that, although well-intentioned, risk achieving the same low level of satisfaction—and low level of positive results!—as their antiquated, abandoned antecedents.

What's happened is that in acknowledging the fact that the traditional performance review process has become outmoded, and in seeking its replacement, companies have continued to focus on process, not purpose. They are looking for a better process, a more effective tool, another system, without looking hard enough at the purpose those processes and tools and systems are intended to accomplish.

This is borne out, in dramatic fashion, by recent studies showing that the removal of the hated performance review often resulted in measurable *declines* in productivity and, equally and perhaps even more dire, manager to employee communication. Something's being overlooked here. As companies look for and test different approaches to replacing the traditional evaluation, they're continuing to overlook what was wrong with the formal performance review in the first place. Replacing one ineffective tool or process with another ultimately ineffective tool or process isn't progress, and it certainly isn't revolutionary.

I would never argue that processes and tools, methodologies and procedures aren't important aspects of operationally effective companies and organizations. I run a company and I know first-hand the necessity and importance of system and methodology. As you'll see in the course of this book, there is a strong methodology to my approach to the **feedback revolution.**

But it's a methodology, not a straightjacket.

Because I also know, same as you, that the place for systematic, standardized approaches is in the systematic elements of the business. The attempt to extend systematization to employee evaluation ignores the fact that employees—and managers—aren't systems.

They're *people*, and rather than expend time, effort and investment in other attempts to create a 21st century version of the traditional performance review in the form of an app, or perform cosmetic surgery and preserve the review by calling it an "evaluation conversation," the time has come to focus on the *purpose* of manager to employee communications.

That purpose is not, of course, to produce a numerical or qualitative rating of the employee's productivity and performance achievements and areas in need of improvement, those ratings-sheets to be passed up the line and filed away in a personnel file.

The real purpose is to ensure that the employee understands her or his strengths, areas for improvement, and contribution to the task at-hand and the company as a whole—her or his *value*, not just evaluation. And that understanding must be communicated, reinforced and adapted to changing circumstances and contexts *constantly.*

I've made some sharp comments in this chapter about the error of replacing the formal performance review with regularly scheduled "performance conversations." My skepticism about the effectiveness of these conversations flows less from their nature, and certainly not from their intent, than from the sense that the conversations should be elements in an evaluation procedure, another *pro forma* approach to employee communication.

The problem is one of mindset, not purpose.

A decade or so ago, a friend who was an executive with Western Union, told me that he spent a portion of every Friday thinking about each of his direct reports. He considered not just their skills and performance in their job, but also what their career goals were, what hopes and dreams drove them, how they were progressing toward achieving those hopes and dreams, how he could help them make progress, and where he could show them how to improve.

My friend's approach focused on the direct reports as *people* and, as he told me, that focus served to remind him that *people* are what his job, and every manager's job, is all about. He was a better manager because he spent that time every week thinking about *them*, not himself.

The fact that he did this regularly each Friday, was a discipline and a *commitment*, not a scheduled evaluation requirement. The insights and ideas he generated during those Friday thinking-sessions enabled him to provide better, more effective, and most importantly, *personalized* feedback to his direct reports.

Commitment to the personal is, as this book will unfold, at the heart of the **feedback revolution**, as my Western Union friend knew a decade ago.

In short, the staid, antiquated and ineffective, filed-and-forgotten performance review is best replaced with dynamic and highly effective personal feedback, personally and individually crafted and delivered on an ongoing and near-constant basis. In order to do that, we have to first re-think and in some ways reinvent what we think feedback is, and how we go about providing—and receiving—it.

That's what the **feedback revolution** is all about.

For the **feedback revolution** to be effective and worthwhile, we first need to examine what effective feedback really is—and in doing so discover, as the next chapter shows, that much of what we've thought about feedback has been off-base and some of it outright wrong.

But we'll also be looking at what's right about our attitudes toward feedback and how, with a few adjustments in approach and follow-through, we can begin creating a true **feedback revolution** that delivers truly positive results up and down the lines of communication in our organizations.

TWO

To Give Effective Feedback You Need to Know What Effective Feedback Is— And Isn't

It's all very well to speak of replacing ineffective, static, scheduled formal reviews and evaluations with dynamic, lively and productive conversations, dialogues, and communications. For those replacements to work, they must be built around a central, indispensable, constantly practiced and ultimately mastered element . . .

Feedback!

Which should come as no surprise.

Even before you picked up and opened this book, there's a good chance that you've encountered the word in the context of replacing or evolving your evaluation systems.

In fact, "Feedback" is mentioned so constantly in the press coverage and commentary, in management seminars and consulting reports, that it runs the risk of becoming just another piece of jargon, one more buzzword added to the mix. Another bit of . . . *noise.*

That's a shame—and it becomes much more than a shame when those evaluation/review-replacement strategies fail because too little attention was paid to the *content* of those conversations, dialogues and communications. Without deeply and fully addressing the nature of effective feedback, and specifically what *makes* it effective, those strategies are more likely to fail than succeed. Simply saying, "We're going to add more feedback to our employee communications," actually says next to nothing. The right and necessary questions haven't been asked.

What are those questions? Let's take the most important one first:

- **What do I mean by "Feedback?"**

I'm not the world's biggest fan of negative examples, but let me take a moment to tell you a few things that real feedback isn't:

- **Real feedback isn't a lecture.**

- **Real feedback isn't a "chewing-out."**

- **Real feedback isn't compliments or praise.**

- **Real feedback isn't a pay raise (or lack of one).**

- **Real feedback isn't a generic and impersonal "attaboy" or "you need to do better."**

- **Real feedback isn't a "bitch session"—it's not even a bull session!**

- **Real feedback doesn't pass the buck, place the blame, or let off steam.**

- **Real feedback isn't saved-up for the next scheduled meeting or conversation.**

- Real feedback isn't a grade on a scale.

- Real feedback isn't a chance to show off, self-aggrandize, win brownie points or earn gratitude.

- Real feedback isn't something you provide because you're expected to; real feedback isn't an item on a check-off list of management responsibilities.

- Real feedback isn't a demand, a command or a reprimand.

Had enough negatives? I have. And if you're like me, you have spent enough time in business to have experienced bad or less-than-thoughtful managers and superiors, you could probably put together a list twice as long as the one I just offered.

My point is that without giving serious, careful, and in-depth thought and reflection to the nature of the feedback you'll be giving (and receiving), you're already in the position of treating your new approach to employee evaluation and development as a mechanical, *pro forma* exercise. Your "feedback" will carry no genuine content—it *will* carry large, unwanted, and generally negative consequences.

Sound familiar? What is generally considered to be feedback is actually just another file-and-forget bit of managerial noise. Clearly none of us set out to create such a situation any more than the original designers of ratings-scale evaluations set out to create the most dreaded piece of procedure in the organization's toolbox.

So how do we avoid condemning our feedback to this un-wanted fate?

As the title suggests, we *revolutionize* our thinking about what real feedback is, how it's crafted, how it's presented and deliv-ered, and how it's practiced on a constant and daily basis.

THINK! It's an Even Better Motto for Feedback Than it is for IBM!

My friend, writer and editor Keith Ferrell, has a story he likes to tell in his speeches to corporate and other audience types. It goes something like this:

At the end of the semester a teacher stood before his class, a stack of marked-up and graded term papers ready to be returned to the students. Staring for a moment at the student's faces—all eager to get their papers back and get on with more important matters like summer vacation—the teacher chose his words carefully.

"You've each had a full semester to gather research and write your papers. After reading them, I want to compliment you on your accomplishments. You're all, as it turns out, smarter than I am."

The students actually perked up at that. It was the first time the teacher had seen interest on their faces in weeks, and he savored the moment before continuing.

"You see," he said before beginning to return the papers, "unlike you, I've always found it necessary, or at least helpful, to *think* before *I* begin to write."

The point of Keith's story—in addition to the laughter it receives from his audiences—is that the students would undoubtedly see the red marks and low grades as the teacher's feedback on their work, a situation familiar to any of us who've endured a ratings-scale performance review. But the real feedback delivered pointedly and gently by the teacher was the importance of *thought* before writing.

Keep that in mind the next time you receive a bit of communication that seemingly has nothing to say and gives no evidence that its author gave any thought at all to what he or she wasn't saying. And this should be at the top of your mind if *you're* the one behind the communication!

Let's take another look at that definition of feedback that I showed you at the beginning of the book:

> *Feedback is information that is shared with a person or group for the distinct purpose of improving results or relationships. Effective feedback is not venting, blaming, shaming or yielding to excuses.*

Having worked hard, along with Peter McLaughlin and other members of our team to develop that definition, I'm proud of every word it contains. There are three words that stand out for me, and do so because I find them missing from most of what is labeled "feedback" in the business world.

The first is: INFORMATION

Every piece of effective feedback has important information at its heart. There is a specific message, containing clearly presented and comprehensible information, being delivered to the feedback recipient.

The second is: PURPOSE

In other words, you have a *reason* for delivering feedback, whatever the specific nature of that feedback may be. There is nothing perfunctory or programmatic about either the feedback itself or its presentation to the employee.

The third: IMPROVING

All information shared and resulting discussion is intended for improvement—not for venting, blaming or shaming.

In the course of this book we'll be looking deeply into these aspects of effective feedback. For now ask yourself about a piece of feedback (or what you may have thought was feedback) that you've delivered (or received). Keeping in mind the notion of distinct purpose, answer these questions:

- **What was the information content of the feedback?** Could you make a list, however brief, of the specific information, and its relevance to performance or productivity, that the feedback contained?

- **Why was the feedback given?** Did it address a specific situation or need? Did the feedback make absolutely clear why that situation or need was being addressed? Did you and the recipient—or provider if you were the recipient—both fully understand and agree on the feedback's purpose?

Information and *Distinct Purpose.* Strong, simple words with powerful implications and consequences—and the central effective feedback factors. Only by placing these two factors at the very forefront of *all* of our thinking about feedback, can we begin to create the *feedback revolution* that transforms every aspect of our work place, and the relationships on which those workplaces rest.

As I mentioned, I'm proud of our definition of feedback and I'm confident that as you read and absorb this book and its lessons, you will also come to see how accurate a definition of real, *effective* feedback it is. But I also keep in mind a lesson learned long ago about definitions. The definition of *dam* will tell you what one is: a barrier for retaining water or other substances or, more obscurely, the female parent of an animal. Those definitions don't tell you how to build a dam or for that matter, raise and nurture sheep or goats.

Now that we've defined effective feedback, let's spend the rest of the book looking at how to build it, both in terms of specific one-on-one feedback, and in the larger sense of creating, raising and nurturing, a *feedback revolution* within our organizations and their cultures.

THREE

Feedback's Five Fundamentals

It should be clear that effective and worthwhile feedback consists of more than just words. In fact, in developing the *iLove-Feedback*® training program, we identified five essential elements that shape, guide, and enrich feedback.

There is plenty of well-documented and clinical evidence that feedback, properly crafted and consistently presented, generates large and measurable positive returns in:

- **Employee productivity**
- **Employee morale**
- **Employee comprehension of company purpose and goals**
- **Employee retention**
- **Employee ability and willingness to communicate with managers/supervisors**

Any one of these goals is desirable and *every* one of them, in my experience and the experiences of the scores of managers and executives with whom I've worked and spoken, is a mission-critical quality *in need of dramatic improvement*. Effective, consistent, and specific feedback delivers these improvements across-the-board.

But—and it's not a small one—the key lies in the *nature* of the feedback and its presentation, *not* in the decision to simply increase the amount of feedback employees receive.

Transforming that situation and persuading ourselves, our managers and employees that there's more to feedback than an occasional sit-down talk with employees, demands that we give the implementation of effective feedback as much practice and skill refinement as we would with any introduction of a new element into our organization's culture. The goal, as with all new elements or initiatives, is to transform, not disrupt, to enrich, not restrict. In short, we have to revolutionize not just the role and prevalence of feedback in our culture, also our sense of what constitutes effective feedback.

I've shared our feedback definition with you a couple of times now. As I mentioned on previous pages, I'm well-aware that it *is* a definition, not a blueprint roadmap. It simply tells you what effective feedback *is*. Now, let's talk about how to achieve it. That's where my five feedback fundamentals come into play.

The five fundamentals of effective feedback are:

1. *Create and nurture your feedback zone*—a specific state of mind, attitude, understanding and outlook that prepares you to develop and deliver the most effective feedback possible.

2. *Think before you give feedback*—think specifically, engaging your empathy and intuition, as well as your managerial skills and business/employee goals, preparing and rehearsing (if only in your mind) the feedback you will be giving.

3. *Learn the language of effective feedback*—the language you use, as well as the tone you employ, will determine the effectiveness of your feedback message. Learn to

avoid ambiguity and judgmental language, and cultivate your mastery of specific language communicating observable details.

4. *Ask permission before giving feedback*—effective feedback is a conversation and a dialogue, not a monologue or lecture. By asking permission to present your feedback message, you are both showing your employee the respect that she or he deserves, and also, crucially, issuing an implied invitation for the employee to participate in the feedback conversation.

5. *Feedback involves both follow-up and follow-through*— unlike annual performance reviews and other static employee communications and interactions, a genuine feedback process doesn't stop as soon as the initial feedback conversation is ended. Effective and worthwhile feedback is virtually always a starting point, not a culmination.

To Thine Own Feedback Be True!

To be honest, giving ourselves effective, worthwhile feedback is probably impossible. But that doesn't mean it's a waste of time to try . . .

As a good manager you're attuned to the individual nature of each of your direct reports or employees (and probably have a better-than-good-sense of the natures of your colleagues and, especially, your own managers or supervisors). Understanding their nature—and that the people you manage are just that, *people*—their ambitions, hopes and dreams outside the company, as well as their career paths, will prove invaluable as you begin revolutionizing your approach to feedback.

But what about yourself? How often, when reviewing your own performance, whether in a formal self-appraisal, or just running through things in your mind as you drive home after work, do you give yourself actual feedback? And how often is your "feedback" to yourself something along the lines of:

- I should have done _____
- I really screwed that up!
- How am I going to fix this?
- What was I thinking?

Or your own personal variation on kicking yourself.

Some days of course, your self-evaluation may take the form of:

- I'm a Superstar!
- Nailed it!
- No stopping me now!
- I'm going to spend my bonus on _____

In neither case are you giving yourself actual, effective, worthwhile *feedback*.

As you read this book and as your approach to effective feedback continues to take shape, try applying the lessons and feedback fundamentals to how you talk with yourself on those homeward drives. Take a moment before starting your car—or boarding an airplane—and put yourself in your feedback zone. Give some thought to whatever the situation or context you're reflecting upon, be specific in the language you use when considering your performance, and give yourself permission (yeah, I know how it sounds, but you get my drift), and plan to follow-up on your internal review. Like I said, there may be a limit to how objective this approach to yourself can be. It's *guaranteed* to be more effective, and ultimately far more productive, than simply kicking yourself or indulging in wildly overblown self-praise.

Try it—you just may like it!

We'll be looking at each of these in far greater detail over the next five chapters. Notice that these five fundamentals of effective feedback are free from jargon and by-the-numbers process and procedure. They are not however, either individually or collectively, "directives" detailing how feedback must be structured, how often it is to be delivered, what number of factors must be addressed in each feedback conversation, or any other stricture. Rather, what these fundamentals do is provide a carefully thought-out, thoroughly tested and proven framework for you to absorb and make your own. They are a set of tools and frankly, a mindset. (I know I promised to avoid jargon, but sometimes the right word is the right word, and *mindset* is the right word here.)

Just as you, me and undoubtedly all of us have encountered from time-to-time the "my way or the highway," and "this is how it's done because *I* say this is how it's to be done" management approaches and structures that chafe and imprison us, you would also scoff at a strict and inflexible approach to feedback.

Believe me—there's nothing revolutionary about an imposed structure aimed at eliminating all variables and, whether it says so overtly or not, individuality from our feedback. We're not robots and neither are our employees, direct reports, or colleagues. You give feedback to a robot by reprogramming it or turning it off. You provide feedback to a person by engaging with her or him in a shared conversation.

That said, my approach to revolutionary feedback isn't an unstructured "do-your-own-thing" bit of "fluff-philosophy" either. The *feedback revolution*, as developed by our team is actually a wide-ranging and comprehensive *discipline*, as rigorous and exhaustive as any worthwhile management initiative. Note that I said *exhaustive*, in the sense of being comprehensive and both applicable and adaptable to every situation, not *exhausting* (in the sense of, "What corporate hoops do they want me to jump through *now*?").

Put into practice and nurtured within your organization, you will find, generally quickly and in some cases right-away, that a commitment to feedback—real, effective, and revolutionary feedback—will enliven and energize everyone involved in the feedback chain. You will also find, as your *feedback revolution* becomes a fully-fledged and self-reinforcing feedback culture, that the chain extends and stretches until it touches every aspect of your organization.

Best of all, you'll discover that the feedback chain is one chain that liberates, not imprisons.

After a brief Interlude, we'll look more closely, one-at-a-time, at our five feedback fundamentals, and how you can make each of them your own.

INTERLUDE

From Paul Revere to Peyton Manning: In Feedback, Timeliness is King!

In his book *The Tipping Point*, Malcolm Gladwell cites a story about Paul Revere paying stable boys to give him daily reports about any changes in the movement of the British troops. Revere figured that if there were going to be any attacks on the American militia, they would start with the British "saddling up."

While sitting in the tavern with his fellow revolutionaries (the tavern was Paul Revere's office, as it has been the office of most of history's great revolutionaries), the word came from the stable that the British were getting ready to ride.

As Gladwell puts it, Paul Revere "was the logical one to go to if you were a stable boy on the afternoon of April 18, 1775 and overheard two British officers talking about how there would be hell to pay on the following day."

Armed with the information the stable boys provided, Paul Revere set out for Lexington that night—and the famous **"Midnight Ride of Paul Revere"** entered history and legend.

One might say that the Revolutionary War was won by the American revolutionists because of "timely feedback" and not the dated feedback of the British. Always having to go across the ocean for permission on any big assaults or decisions eliminated one of the most vital elements of effective feedback—*timeliness*.

Switch to modern-day "Wars of the NFL" and look at the Denver Broncos' Peyton Manning, certainly one of the greatest quarterbacks of all time. And yet, after 14 seasons in the NFL, he feels that he still needs people giving him advice and helping him maintain a fresh attitude and new ideas; he too, pays for feedback. (Technically the Broncos organization paid Adam Gase, his former quarterback coach and now the offensive coordinator, to give him specific and unceasing feedback.)

As Peyton said in the Denver Post (9/15/12), "I think the older you get, the more important it is to have a guy to watch your fundamentals, certainly go over defenses and reads and progressions, but also to go over your fundamentals, your throwing mechanics."

But Peyton Manning also knows how to *give* feedback, a skill never more on display than in the October 15, 2012 game against San Diego when he led his team back from a scoreless first half, 0-24, to a 35-24 double-digit victory. It was the first time in NFL history that had been accomplished. Still settling into his role as quarterback for the Broncos, Manning used feedback to guide his teammates' responses and patterns to plays he called, showing them what *he* wanted, how *he* does it, all while giving them plenty of positives for the performances his feedback was reshaping. The results speak for themselves—and so now do the NFL records.

Now, think of Peyton Manning as a manager of your company. If the way he studies his teammates is any indication, he would know all the tendencies of his direct reports, their strengths and weaknesses, and he would ask for *their* feedback to help him communicate more effectively with them. From the feedback of the top brass, he would know the direction the enterprise is moving and would, in turn, give feedback to his team so they (like his offensive line) would know their parts as participants in the grand scheme.

If, like Paul Revere, we would seek out feedback and, like Peyton Manning, we would put aside our own egos and anxieties about receiving and giving on-time feedback, our own *"Feedback Revolution"* would be off to a great start.

FOUR

Finding and Maintaining Your Feedback Zone

We've all experienced the "bad day effect" that occurs when a manager or supervisor is having a "bad day," and her or his mood spills into communications, commentary or conversations with us. Some and perhaps most of us have even been guilty of this ourselves. And we've *all* experienced something like this during those late, unlamented formal performance reviews. Nobody liked them, and only rarely were the reviews greeted with enthusiasm by either reviewer or recipient.

We all have bad days. But when communicating with colleagues and subordinates, it is essential that external factors, and internal moods or distractions, be kept in their place. That place is far from the space where you are communicating with others in your organization.

This is especially true of feedback.

Feedback, as I've pointed out, is most effective when it is positive, even when the feedback addresses and seeks to correct a critical problem or workplace issue. And while it seems both obvious and self-evident, it's important to bear in mind that it's hard, even impossible, to deliver positive feedback when your thoughts are colored or preoccupied with other matters.

Likewise, we should seek to be aware of external factors that might be affecting the recipient's workplace performance, shaping the feedback we intend to deliver. The "bad day effect" can affect a subordinate's ability to *receive* feedback just as surely as our bad days can affect our ability to deliver a positive message.

The solution?

Find and nurture your *Feedback Zone.*

ZONED FOR FEEDBACK

What *is* the Feedback Zone?

Quite simply, the Feedback Zone is you and your state as you prepare, deliver and follow-up on feedback. By your *state* I mean the combination of your:

- *Energy*

- *Attitude*

- *Environment*

Achieving a proper balance among these elements will help you establish the right state of mind, emotion and mood for the feedback you are preparing to present. Obviously, each of these elements possesses a variety of qualities that you must be aware of, with special attention paid to how these qualities might be affected by the situation or context that calls for feedback. Here's a basic inventory of the qualities and characteristics of a Feedback Zone:

ENERGY

- **Are you calm and focused?** Distraction and nervous energy are unwelcome in your Feedback Zone.

- **Have you reviewed the feedback and its context/ cause to ensure that your interpretation is proper and accurate?** If not, you may feel defensive about the feedback you're about to present—and defensiveness is never proper with effective feedback.

- **Has the situation you're addressing caused you any anger, annoyance or hurt?** Have you eliminated or sequestered those emotions from the business purpose of your feedback message?

- **Are you confident in your ability to present your feedback message clearly, cogently and positively?**

- **Are you physically rested, mentally sharp?**

ATTITUDE

- **Are you approaching the feedback session determined to deliver a message of *improvement*, not just to point out a problem or issue?**

- **Is the purpose of your feedback message to ensure that there is no element of blame, shame or retribution involved?** Feedback is a professional tool—and your feedback's words and tone must reflect that professionalism.

- **Does your feedback include preparation and your willingness to assist the recipient achieve the positive goals the feedback establishes?**

- **Are you prepared to be candid with the recipient, delivering the message without "sugar-coating" while also maintaining grace and positive demeanor?**

- **Do you have facts and documentation to support your feedback?** Effective feedback is *always* specific.

ENVIRONMENT

- **Is the feedback being presented in a timely fashion?**
Effective feedback is always timely. Peter McLaughlin liked to point out that like good, opened wine, feedback doesn't store well. Be sure to take enough time to get all aspects of your Feedback Zone in order, but don't procrastinate or delay delivering your feedback message.

- **Will your feedback be presented in an appropriate location, away from distractions, including co-workers?**
Feedback is private, not a performance.

- **Have you considered and selected the right time of day (for you and the recipient) for a feedback session?**

- **If the feedback is a follow-up on an earlier conversation, are you prepared to recap the earlier session in order to make certain that you and the recipient are "up-to-speed?"**

- **If you can't have a face-to-face meeting with the recipient, how will you present your feedback: Telephone conversation? Video conference? Email or messaging exchange?**

Those are the basic elements of a healthy Feedback Zone. As you can see, there are congruencies and crossovers among the various items in the three elements. This is by design; the qualities of effective feedback reinforce and nourish each other. If you're rested and calm, for instance, you're better prepared to evaluate and assemble the other ingredients of your feedback message.

CARE AND FEEDING OF YOUR FEEBACK ZONE

Clearly, none of us can master all of a Feedback Zone's qualities without practice and discipline. In fact, practice and discipline themselves could easily be included in this inventory. But there *are* approaches to establishing the basics of your Feedback Zone, establishing a solid foundation for it, and building upon that foundation.

- **Calmness and focus are appropriate for *all* business situations, not just feedback sessions.** In other words, "Put on your own oxygen mask first." If you're calm and focused in day-to-day operations, you'll be calm and focused when feedback is called for.

- **Cultivating timeliness in all dealings with co-workers and subordinates extend naturally to providing feedback on a timely basis.**

- **Look for the positive throughout the business day.** This doesn't mean putting on rose-colored glasses or a Pollyanna persona. Rather, a constant emphasis on seeking the positive will not only help you cast your feedback in positive terms, it will also enhance all other phases of your work life.

- **Watch your energy levels and make sure you're getting plenty of rest.** Taking the same advice your doctor would give you about your work will make it easier for you to assess your own physical state when preparing to deliver crucial feedback.

In short, your Feedback Zone is a specifically targeted discipline that reflects the sort of mental, physical and emotional balance and equilibrium that are in many ways ideal for all areas of our professional and personal lives. Ideal, but not *idealized*. The inventory of qualities necessary for a working Feedback Zone are realistic, reasonable and achievable. The more you put your Feedback Zone into practice, the more natural it will feel, and the more easily entered it will be when feedback times and situations arise.

By the time you've grown familiar and comfortable with finding and entering your Feedback Zone, you will also be more easily able to recognize and adjust or self-correct those areas where your Zone is drifting or risks going off-track. Recognizing those potential missteps is itself an important part of mastering your Feedback Zone.

In the next chapter we'll begin to look at how you incorporate your Feedback Zone into the practice of giving positive, effective feedback in the work environment.

FIVE

Getting Smart About Feedback

One of the largest differences between traditional performance reviews and our new and revolutionary approach to feedback is that for the new approach to feedback to work, it must be a *conscious* process at every step.

We can all admit that annual performance reviews rarely met that criteria, more often than not, they gave the impression that the scores and checked-off boxes had been hastily entered, probably after a long period of delay and avoidance.

Feedback doesn't work that way.

It can't.

Creating and delivering effective and worthwhile feedback is, perhaps above all, a *thoughtful* process. And that thoughtful process will draw upon all of your thought *processes*. Those thought processes, in turn, are guided and shaped by various internal and external filters that affect how you see, interact and respond to the world around you.

We all have these filters, developed over our lifetimes, with the result that each of us responds to the world in different, unique ways. Sometimes those differences are tiny, other times huge. You can see these filters at work in, for example, the radically different responses you and a friend may have to the same joke. One of you may laugh uproariously, the other not even chuckle.

More seriously, think about how your filters touch upon and shape your relationships at work. One of the keys to crafting effective feedback is to recognize that while your message will be affected by your own filters, how the message is received will be affected by the recipient's perceptual filters. Among the filters that should be considered as you begin to prepare a feedback message are:

- **Social and cultural environment and background**
- **Gender**
- **Generational differences**
- **Hierarchy and perceived power structure**
- **Skill level**
- **Emotions**
- **Values**

You will be thinking about, and examining carefully, your internal and external filters, to ensure that they are not inadvertently compromising the quality and value of the feedback you are considering. In other words, you will be making sure that your feedback message not only embodies the message you seek to deliver, it has been shaped and adjusted to minimize any unwanted effects of your personal filters.

In order to safeguard your feedback, and guarantee that it is effective and achieves the desired results, you must engage these processes before creating the feedback message. That means in addition to the business purposes and considerations that prompt the feedback, you must:

- **Ask Why**

  - Why am I giving this feedback?

  - Why do I feel that this person needs this particular feedback now?

- **Ask What**

  - What do I want to accomplish with the feedback?

  - What do I want the recipient to take away from this feedback?

- **Ask How**

  - How will I deliver this feedback?

  - How will I ensure that the recipient views the feedback as a positive action, not as simple criticism?

- **Ask When**

  - When is the soonest time that I can have the feedback prepared, in order to ensure its timeliness?

  - When will I actually deliver the feedback—what is the best time of day or week for a feedback conversation?

Your recipient's response to the feedback will be affected by her or his unique internal and external filters. Combat this by arming yourself with the knowledge of these filters by being aware of:

- **Your knowledge of the person's work history**

- **Your interactions with the person in the workplace**

- **Notations in the personnel file or on performance reviews (if your company still has them)**

- **Comments from other workers or managers**

You will need to ask yourself if any of these factors have affected your thinking in inappropriate or undesirable ways. Are the comments you've heard legitimate observations, or biased sniping? Should past (and perhaps long-past) file comments from previous managers have any relevance to the feedback situation and context at-hand?

As you answer these questions, and cycle through any issues or potential problems those answers may raise, keep an eye on the clock/calendar. Effective feedback is always timely. Don't spend so much time asking yourself questions that you neglect to prepare and deliver the feedback while its context and goals are still fresh. You will find that the process of getting smart about feedback takes less and less time as you become more and more accustomed to, and experienced with, the process.

©CARTOONBANK.COM

"Never, ever, think outside the box."

Unlike the formal review, whose elements were often guided by antiquated policies or a committee meeting resolution, one of which convened decades ago, this approach to feedback is by its nature rooted in the present. You won't be referring to formal review guidelines and scoring schedules. Rather, your focus will be placed on a current situation or practice in need of feedback, and guiding the creation of that feedback with your own sense of yourself as a manager or co-worker, of the recipient and her or his individual characteristics, and the current nature of the business and workplace environment.

With those in mind, you will be able to tailor your feedback in such a way that it meets both your needs to deliver a specific message and letting the recipient know that your feedback is a positive and personalized contribution to her or his performance within the organization. In fact, I have found that the process of getting smart about feedback becomes second-nature after only a few feedback sessions.

Instead of working through a checklist and reminding yourself of the various elements you need to consider when preparing feedback, you will quickly reach the point where you would no more undertake to deliver feedback without assembling these elements, than you would step out into a rainstorm without an umbrella or raincoat.

Getting smart and staying smart about feedback provides an additional benefit over and beyond addressing and improving the immediate feedback situation at-hand. Getting smart about feedback not only reinforces itself within you, it tends to spread by example to others in your organization. Once your direct reports experience your positive, specific and timely feedback approach a couple of times, they will begin formulating their own approach based on these experiences when they come to you with questions, suggestions and feedback of their own.

SIX

Crafting the Feedback Message

You have established and entered your Feedback Zone, gotten smart about the person receiving the feedback and are informed about the context of the circumstance that prompted the feedback.

Now all you have to do is get together with the recipient and deliver the feedback, right?

Wrong.

Your next step is to create the precise feedback message you want to deliver. Effective feedback is more than knowing what has to be said and what points must be communicated in order to address the matter at hand. You also must know how you're going to make those points.

All the preparation in the world won't make your feedback effective if you enter the feedback session without a specific understanding of the message your recipient is to receive.

Generalities or vague and ambiguous comments can do more harm than good. For your feedback to be effective, your message itself must be effective. And that means that it must be:

- **Clearly worded, reflecting thoughtful attention paid to word-choice and phrasing**

- **Specific, containing the necessary amount of detail and documentation**
- **Non-judgmental**
- **Open, honest and candid**
- **Positive in tone**
- **Welcoming and encouraging dialogue**

In other words, your feedback language must be as smart and as carefully thought-out in its delivery as it is in every other aspect of its preparation.

©CARTOONBANK.COM

"Keep up the good work, whatever it is, whoever you are."

CLARITY COUNTS

We've all experienced so-called feedback that's so general or poorly-phrased that it says less than nothing:

- **"You're doing great."**
- **"You're doing poorly."**

- "You need to improve."
- "You could be more productive."
- "I like what you're doing."
- "You could do your job better."

None of those comments provide the recipient with anything more than a vague sense of how their performance is perceived by the speaker. Additionally, and not incidentally, each of the phrases is fundamentally judgmental.

Now look at how careful phrasing and word-choice transforms each of the vague phrases into an opening that clearly sets the stage for delivery of specific feedback:

- "I'm impressed with how you've met or exceeded your numbers this quarter, and would like to talk with you about how you accomplished this."

- "I'd like to talk with you about the decline in your numbers over the past few weeks, and how we can work together to turn things around."

- "Knowing you, I know that you're interested in improving your performance, and would like to discuss with you things we can do to make that happen."

- "I believe that if we work together we can increase your productivity and do so in ways that make your job more rewarding and enjoyable."

- "I want to say what a pleasure it is to work with someone as consistently prepared and on-target as you."

- "We should talk about some ideas I have concerning ways your job could be more engaging and make better use of your talents and skills."

While none of those phrases contain specific, detailed insight into the matter that called for the feedback, each of the phrases does let the recipient know, easily and naturally, that there is a specific matter being discussed.

Those specifics will, of course, be the heart of the feedback itself.

EFFECTIVE FEEDEBACK IS SPECIFIC

Building outward from your clearly-worded opening, you will craft your message around the specific and observed behavior that produced the need for feedback in the first place. Rather than, for instance, vague words or phrases such as:

- **Often**
- **Lots**
- **Frequently**
- **Several**
- **Many**

. . . develop specific language based on the observed and documented information:

- **70% percent of your time**
- **Five instances of**
- **Twice a week**
- **Four of our clients**
- **Fourteen deliveries were mislabeled**

By grounding the feedback in real-world, observed performance details, you're letting the employee know that the discussion is being held to work on an identified issue, not a general "sense" that something needs to change. Your documentation and specific information are intended to bring clarity to the conversation and provide focus for the feedback, not to present the recipient with a dossier in support of a prosecution.

It's equally important that the person receiving the feedback understands that the information you've gathered is a normal part of workplace process, observation and methodology, and not a deliberate search for "Gotcha!" material.

JUDGE NOT, LEST—

Feedback is never judgmental.

We looked earlier at the sorts of word-choices that send an immediate—and often ineradicable—message of judgment, whether positive or negative. That's not the purpose of feedback. The purpose of feedback is to accomplish specific improvements, and to do so from a positive posture, and without judgment.

Judgmental language also reinforces hierarchies. Now clearly your feedback session is not intended to diminish or weaken your managerial role. Just as clearly, in terms of effective feedback, a worthwhile feedback session should be a conversation and dialogue, not a lecture to a captive audience. Be alert for judgmental language throughout the feedback session.

HONESTY REALLY IS THE BEST

Openness and honesty are crucial components of effective feedback—and of an effective, productive and efficient workplace. If you're attentive to the elements of effective feedback, and disciplined about putting those elements into practice with your own employees and peers, you will find that openness and honesty are all but automatically built into your feedback preparation.

You will be approaching feedback not through rose-colored glasses, but clear-eyed and ready to address the issue at hand in open, candid terms, while setting a tone that will be matched in return by your employee or colleague. In this way, your honest and open approach to creating a feedback message that is authentic, open and candid, and reflects those qualities in every word, plays a strong part in establishing and encouraging an honest and open workplace beyond the specific parameters and content of the feedback session. Honesty, openness and candor are among the most vital—and most easily noticed—qualities of a feedback culture.

POSITIVELY FEEDBACK

As with honesty and openness, a positive approach is so deeply built into the preparatory phases of a feedback session that you will gravitate toward positive language and tone from the moment you begin crafting the specific message.

The fact that you are using specific information without judgment helps set that positive tone. The body of your message will further reinforce the positive outcomes of the feedback conversation. You will be letting the person receiving the feedback know that you are:

- *Enthusiastic* about them and their potential

- *Confident* that the issue or situation can be addressed in an affirmative manner

- *Helpful* in any way that you can be to the employee

- *Available* to continue developing the ultimately positive result you both seek

CAN WE TALK?

To end this section with the beginning of your feedback conversation may seem odd—but I have my reasons. In the course of developing the *iLoveFeedback®* program, I was reminded more than once of something we all need to remind ourselves:

Feedback sessions involve more than one person.

That is of course as obvious as can be—you wouldn't be having a feedback conversation unless there was a person to whom you need to offer feedback.

Over time, though, it became obvious to me that the key word in that sentence is the one most easily overlooked:

Involve

As we find our Feedback Zone, get smart about ourselves and the person to whom we'll be presenting the feedback, assemble our information and craft our message, it can be all too easy to forget that the recipient of our feedback is more than an audience. He or she is a *participant* in the *feedback process*, not just in receiving the feedback itself. This is a conversation and a dialogue, not the delivery of wisdom writ large and from on-high.

Throughout the feedback session, your honesty, openness and candor must extend to your own willingness and eagerness to hear what the person receiving the feedback has to say. Be ready to listen carefully and to guide, subtly and with encouragement, the recipient to being as specific, candid and open in response and discussion as you have been in the feedback message itself. For most of us, this really is a revolution in performance-related workplace communications. It's a revolution that, once introduced, will prove so effective you'll wonder how any organization could survive without it.

As we'll discuss in the next chapter, the success of that *feedback revolution* rests upon the effectiveness with which you transform your efforts in creating the feedback message into the actual delivery of it.

INTERLUDE

EDGAR ALLAN POE AND SCOTT ADAMS (CREATOR OF DILBERT) UNCOVER THE ELEPHANT IN THE ROOM

I was in discussions recently with a small medical products company. We were speaking of potential projects, but I soon realized that nothing would go forward with the participants because they could not be candid with one another.

As an outsider I could see the "elephant in the room" that the insiders refused to acknowledge.

Thoughts of that failed meeting carried me back to one of the first detective short stories ever written, which I had read in high school:

"The Purloined Letter," by Edgar Allan Poe. ("Purloined," from Middle English, means "stolen.") The letter had been stolen from an unnamed woman's boudoir, to be used for blackmail purposes.

The Prefect of Police, who was having no luck finding the letter, called in amateur detective Auguste Dupin to help find it before embarrassing damage could be done. They had a suspect in mind and had searched his hotel room. The French police had looked behind the wallpaper, under the carpet, examined the furniture (with a microscope no less), and had no success.

The next day, Dupin, having found the missing letter in no time and with very little effort, presented it to the Prefect of Police. He explained to the Prefect that the thief was not only clever, he was also aware of standard police procedures. He knew that the police would look for an *elaborate* hiding place, and therefore he had hidden the letter in plain sight...

Dupin had found the letter precisely where no one had looked— in the letter box hanging on the wall, for anyone to see.

Many times, it is the amateur or the outsider who discovers the "elephant in the room" or in this case, the stolen letter sitting in plain sight in the "outgoing mail."

The *feedback revolution* is a new way for us all to become "amateur detectives" and become aware of what is all around us and nobody sees...until now.

Scott Adams, like Poe, uses a character to open the eyes of anyone paying attention. Drawing upon his years as a bank teller (among other jobs), Adams exposes what is really going on in poorly run companies, and then reveals his thoughts through Dilbert and his assemblage of other cartoon characters.

Mark Twain once remarked that HUMOR IS BASED ON GRIEVANCE.

Dilbert brings most of the grievances we experience in our jobs and careers to light in sudden and stunning ways. He has a number of cartoons on feedback, which point out everything that's wrong and yet is still pervasive in most corporate cultures.

One cartoon has Dilbert returning a performance review nine months late and yet all he had done was sign what his direct report herself had written...he completes the second shot of the combination punch by adding that he didn't actually remember if he had even read it.

Another example shows him congratulating a worker for his good work yet telling the same person that he had given him "poor" in the performance review write-up...in case he should ever have to fire him.

In yet a third cartoon panel, Dilbert talks of an employee "accused of unspecified shortcomings by a person who shall remain nameless." The accuser, of course, has been placed in a witness protection program adding to the absurdity of it all, which points to the reality.

SEVEN

Special Delivery: Communicating the Feedback Message

Feedback doesn't exist in a vacuum. Every step of our feedback journey so far has involved both interior thought and reflection, and external observation and documentation. It has been a disciplined, candid process, and until the moment you let the employee or colleague know that you have some feedback to offer, it is a process that takes place within your own thoughts and notes.

Now the time has come to deliver the feedback to the recipient—from this point onward, feedback and various levels and degrees of follow-up and follow-through will be external activities. The conversation is about to begin.

And it begins by asking the recipient for permission.

MAY I?

The simple act of asking permission to give feedback changes and enriches the feedback dynamic in numerous ways.

- **Effective feedback is always *timely*.** Requesting permission to deliver feedback sends the recipient a subtle and immediate signal of timeliness: the feedback you wish to provide will be helpful *now*.

- **Effectively delivered and successfully received feedback requires respect from both parties.** Even the toughest feedback becomes more readily accepted when you've prepared the ground with a simple, respectful request for permission.

- **Feedback is not (or shouldn't be) a lecture or monologue.** Asking permission is an act of issuing an invitation as well as demonstrating respect. You are letting the recipient know upfront that you're initiating a conversation, not unleashing a harangue.

- **Even the most difficult feedback should be delivered in a positive manner.** Few things establish a positive framework for delivering feedback as quickly as asking permission. Your request sets the tone for whatever follows.

- **Feedback is the "human" face of performance evaluation and review.** Rather than an impersonal (and usually ineffective) by-the-numbers checkbox form, feedback is personal. Asking permission to deliver the feedback makes a personal point even before the feedback session begins.

The advantages of asking permission to deliver feedback are by now, I hope, obvious to you. But in the course of developing the *iLoveFeedback®* training program, and writing *Feedback Revolution*, I've become aware of just how unexpected, if not outright alien, feedback permission requests may be to some of you. Let me take a moment to answer the two most common objections I've encountered.

- **Asking permission undermines my managerial authority.** Far from it. Think about the worst manager or boss you ever had. Odds are she or he *never* asked your permission for giving feedback (or, most likely, much of anything else). Now think how different the experiences would have been if your superior had offered a simple, respectful and positive request for permission preceding those exchanges. I'm not saying that a few words or a request would change a bad boss into a great one but, as the old joke goes, it sure couldn't hurt!

- **How can I give tough, but necessary, feedback after I've asked permission?** The question implies, probably without meaning to, that your tough feedback is going to be presented in a manner that's incongruent with asking permission. If so, the issue is with how you're going to present the feedback, not with asking permission to present it. The permission request sets the positive tone: the feedback, even (and perhaps especially) tough feedback, should be shaped to match that tone.

The point is that your request for permission is itself a bit of feedback from you to the employee. It lets them know you consider her or him an important part of your organization. Your feedback will not only be more effectively received, the fact that you asked permission first will be appreciated—and remembered. The *feedback revolution* moves us further from the rigid, scheduled, impersonal and formal performance reviews.

In addition to serving as the primary means of communication, reinforcement, evaluation and adjustment, effective feedback sets a tone of open, human communication, cooperation and understanding that will flow from the specific feedback event to inform, enhance and improve all areas of performance.

Don't Take "No" for an Answer: And Do So From a Positive Position

What if the intended recipient says "No" to my request for a feedback session?

That's one of the most common queries I receive. I imagine the query is posed more often than the situation actually occurs in the workplace. This is itself a good reminder that even as we adopt and adapt our revolutionary new approach to feedback, we may retain some of the uncertainty and nervousness that accompanied old-style performance reviews.

Relax! Far more often than not, your enthusiastic, positive request for a feedback session will be accepted without incident. Once your *feedback revolution* begins to become established in your organization's culture, you will often find your requests being accepted with a positive enthusiasm on the part of the recipient.

But if you *do* encounter resistance to your request, your response should be firm, while maintaining the positive energy and tone that are the hallmarks of effective feedback. Two effective approaches to overcoming the resistance are:

- **Re-phrase the request.** "If now is not a good time, what would be a better time for you?" *or,* "I believe you will benefit from what I have to say; let's talk about it," are good approaches to overcoming the objection.

- **Be more firm, but remain positive.** With more recalcitrant employees, your words may need to become more firm, though still positive: "I've observed some issues that need to be corrected, and that can be corrected quickly, but to do so I need to give you my feedback now." (You might ask yourself *why* the employee is resistant: there may be other issues than the feedback-specific one that need to be addressed.)

MORE THAN JUST TOKEN APPRECIATION

Once you have asked for and received permission to provide feedback, and have either scheduled or are about to begin the feedback session, take a moment to express your *sincere* appreciation to the employee or colleague for her or his willingness to receive your feedback.

This is neither a perfunctory nor obsequious gesture. The recipient of your feedback thus far has little knowledge about what is coming in the feedback. They will likely be experiencing some level of nervousness, which is perfectly understandable.

Saying a sincere and enthusiastic (without going overboard), "Thank you" accomplishes several things:

- **Your appreciation reinforces the foundation of respect and professionalism that's essential to a feedback conversation.**

- **As you plan your conversation, take time to remind yourself of the other things this person does to contribute to the team.** These attributes make up the whole person and are as important to an effective feedback conversation as the job at hand. The attributes can include expertise, enthusiasm, collaboration efforts and sense of humor. Make sure the recipient knows that you appreciate her or his positive qualities even as you address areas in need of improvement.

- **"Thank you" sends the unmistakable signal that the ensuing conversation is important.**

- **It lets the recipient know that her or his participation in the discussion is not only expected but also appreciated.**

- **It starts the feedback conversation on a *positive* note—** your recipient understands that you have something to discuss and her or his participation in the discussion is something you're looking forward to.

SHARE THE ACTUAL FEEDBACK

I mentioned that the feedback recipient is likely, and understandably, a bit nervous about the feedback session. Bear this in mind as the session gets under way, and be attentive not only to your own body language and tone—open, relaxed, non-accusatory—but also to the recipient's. Be alert for:

- **Defensiveness of tone**

- **Avoiding eye contact**

- **Speaking indistinctly, mumbling**

- **Fidgeting and other signs of nervousness**

- **Failing to answer questions**

- **Resistance, perhaps subtle, to engaging in conversation or dialogue**

Your attentiveness to these and other signals that the feedback recipient isn't fully embracing the *opportunity* the session offers should be met by a renewed and always positive response. Draw the employee or colleague into the conversation with questions:

- **Do you agree with the information I've presented?** And if not, what are *your* impressions of the matter?

- **Have you dealt with changes in performance before?** How did you go about ensuring that those changes were successful, and how can we work together to achieve success in this case?

- **How can *I* help you address these issues?** Are there resources or support that would be helpful to you as we embark on this process of change?

- **Do you feel that *I've overlooked anything in this feedback?***

The goal is to make certain that the employee understands that her or his voice and thoughts are as essential to the feedback session as your own. Reinforce this goal by listening attentively and answering questions specifically, showing the employee or colleague that she or he is being *heard*, not just lectured.

Be alert as well for any negative signals *you* might be sending that your own engagement in the session is less than complete and genuine:

- **Resist the impulse to take too many notes; your attention should be on the recipient of the feedback, not your notepad.**

- **Don't interrupt the recipient when she or he is speaking; listen to everything the recipient has to say.**

- **If the conversation is going off-track, steer it back onto its proper course gently and with encouragement, not cutting the recipient off brusquely.**

PLAN TOGETHER FOR CHANGE TOGETHER

The culmination of the feedback session is the action-plan you and the feedback recipient will put together to ensure that the behavior identified in the feedback conversation is corrected by action in the workplace.

Obviously, that action will differ from situation-to-situation, and there are some proven steps you can take to increase the likelihood of successful change:

- **Involve and engage the recipient in the plan of action; seek her or his input and response to the plan you have developed.**

- **Ask again if there are additional resources and support needed to help the employee successfully make the desired changes.**

- **Prepare a written timeline for follow-up and follow-through, with check-points and interim goals and evaluations/assessments of progress.**

- **Schedule subsequent feedback sessions at specific points.**

- **Make clear that your door is open for inquiries or a discussion as the change process begins and is implemented.**

And as we'll see in the next chapter, end the session well, with enthusiasm and encouragement.

EIGHT

Energy, Encouragement, Attentiveness—Ending Well

If your experiences with formal performance reviews are anything like mine, you know that they all too often simply come to a stop as soon as the reviewer completes all the boxes or numbers on the checklist.

"We're done now," is the reviewer's typical closing comment, generally uttered with a tone of relief. The reviewer may thank you for attending—or may not.

It's like hit and run.

Effective feedback sessions, by design, are inherently different.

As I've shown, every step of the feedback process is aimed at reaching a conclusion where the recipient has received and understood the feedback's content and goals, and is prepared to begin turning the feedback into positive action. This involves more than direct delivery of the feedback message. In fact, while the delivery of the message is the heart of the feedback session, the atmosphere you create to surround and reinforce that message and positive action, is equally important. This atmosphere, like other aspects of effective feedback, should be nourishing, ripe with honestly, openness and candor, allowing the recipient to fully grasp that the message is neither a punishment nor judgment—it's also *not a lecture.*

Creating this type of atmosphere is a crucial aspect of every bit of feedback you deliver. And as the recipients of your feedback become more familiar with your revolutionary approach to feedback, and in turn come to deeply understand this, the benefits of your ***feedback revolution*** will begin to spread and expand.

Of course—there's *always* an "of course"—you can't just *tell* your recipients that you're not giving them a lecture. Some factors come into play here:

- **Based on past experiences with static performance reviews and "getting called to the office," they're not likely to believe you.**

- **If all you do is deliver the feedback followed by a quick dismissal of the recipient, the session is going to seem like a lecture, no matter how noble your intentions.**

The solution resides, as you may have guessed, in *showing* the recipients that real feedback not only helps them, it *involves* them in the actual feedback process itself. And that begins with you letting the recipients know that you—and your resources—are there for them not only as they receive your feedback, also as they transform the feedback into positive action.

> *Feedback is about support—*
> *make sure the recipient knows this.*

The first step in establishing the new approach to feedback with the recipient, then, is to make clear that the feedback session is to be a conversation, and that the recipient's participation is a vital part of the conversation.

As related in the previous chapter, you establish this from the very beginning, the moment when you first inform the recipient of the upcoming session. Remember that even the smallest words can have a large impact here:

"I'd like to talk *to* you about _____"

says, probably without meaning to: "Here comes a lecture."

But:

"I'd like to have a conversation *with* you about _____"

informs the recipient that a conversation will take place and that her or his input will be welcomed. Open and inviting phrasing such as this has laid the groundwork for the conversation.

One of the most important words to avoid is:

Why?

Why communicates or even implies judgment. Asking *why* risks sending the message that this is an interrogation, not a conversation.

Look at the difference in these two approaches to the same question:

Why are you consistently late on deadlines?

. . . puts the employee or colleague in the position of defending themselves—and puts you in the position of an accuser. . . in the recipient's eyes at least!

But

How can we work together to make sure that you don't miss any more deadlines?

or

What can I do to help you meet your deadlines?

. . . are phrasings that let the recipients know you're on *their* side, and have invited them to the feedback session in order to help, and to creative a positive action plan that will transform their behavior. Your phrasing is *supportive,* not judgmental.

Now it's time to build upon that groundwork, and actively encourage a rich and full dialogue about the feedback at hand. Once your basic feedback message has been delivered, your phrasing will remain inviting, and now you are offering direct and specific invitations that not only bring the recipient more deeply into the conversation, but are also aimed at:

- **Assuring the recipient that you are eager to provide the support and resources needed to transform the feedback message into concrete action in the workplace.**

- **You are equally eager to know the recipient's thoughts, insights, attitudes about the feedback you've presented—and how that feedback will be put into positive action.**

You accomplish these purposes with open, supportive questions:

- **"Would it be helpful for me to introduce you to someone who's successfully accomplished this type of change?"**

- **"Tell me about times in the past when you've transformed something (work process, behavior, etc.) in a positive manner."**

- **"Do you foresee any problems or obstacles that will affect your ability to accomplish what we're discussing?**

Tell me about them and let's see how I can help you overcome them."

- **"Now that we've discussed things and established goals, what do _you_ see as your first step, and how can I assist you in taking that step?"**

As you can see, every question is phrased in such a way as to:

- **Encourage dialogue**

- **Reinforce your support and resources**

- **Ensure that the feedback has been understood**

- **Establish next steps**

You've probably noticed something else about the questions:

Once you've asked a question—the next step belongs to the recipient.

When it comes to feedback, silence on your part can be golden.

For feedback to work, you should be listening at least as much (and possibly more) as talking.

LISTEN CAREFULLY

As the saying goes there's a reason we have two ears and only one mouth. The reason is obvious to any of us who have endured a droning performance evaluation lecture (or any other kind of lecture).

Nothing sends a stronger signal that you are interested in and committed to helping your employees or colleagues succeed than showing them that you're interested in hearing what _they_ have to say on the subject. The only way you can do that is by actually *listening.*

And actually listening, means *actively* listening.

TUNING IN TO FEEDBACK

Sometimes you have to fiddle a bit before you "tune in to the feedback station." This was a point—and a metaphor—that was brought home delightfully during an *iLoveFeedback®* program not long ago.

As we reviewed the "Get Smart" step in *iLoveFeedback®*, a lively woman suddenly shouted out: "I get it! I get it!"

What exactly did she get? We all wanted to know, and she was eager to tell us:

"I've been listening to the wrong station!" she exclaimed. "I've been tuned to WIIFM—What's In It For Me!"

Her smile grew even wider as she said: "I need to change to the *right* station: WIIFT—What's In It For *Them!*"

Make sure that your *listening* is attuned to the positive results for the *recipient* of your feedback: you're the station, not the audience.

Active listening means that your sole focus is on the feedback recipient—and the recipient should be aware of this. You should:

- **Stop talking.**
- **Avoid defensiveness when you do talk.**
- **If the recipient poses a question, answer in such a way that shows you respect and understand the reason for the question.**

- **Be attentive to your:**
  - ◆ Eye contact
  - ◆ Body language
  - ◆ Gestures
  - ◆ Tone of voice
  - ◆ Facial expressions
  - ◆ Physical proximity to the other person

Before and during the feedback session, remind yourself (silently) that while feedback is not about hierarchy, your employees or colleagues may not fully understand that yet. Be attentive to *how* they speak and express themselves through eye contact, tone of voice, and so on. While you don't want to send any sort of inappropriate "buddy-buddy, just two pals talking" tone, you do want to keep things on a relaxed and candid conversational level.

ENERGIZE AND END WELL

I don't think I ever actually went to sleep during a long, droning performance review, but there were times when it was close.

Effective feedback sessions have the opposite effect. When you have taken care at every step of the process to craft a message that's precise and specific, to deliver the feedback message in a dynamic, candid and positive way, and to invite the recipient's participation in the feedback conversation, your sessions will be energizing in ways that designers of checklist-based performance reviews could never imagine.

Revolutionary feedback is, as I've shown, about a lot of things. One of the key things it delivers is . . .

Energy!

As the feedback session draws to a close, put that energy to work as you and the recipient map out the next steps. Your priority here is to make sure the employee is prepared to:

- *Address and change* the behavior in question

- *Prepare and review* an action plan with specific next steps and longer-term stages

- *Sustain and extend* the changes beyond the enthusiasm that immediately follows the feedback session

- *Call upon you* when support and encouragement (and more feedback!) is needed

Once the plan is in place and reviewed—including how and at what points the employee's progress will be assessed and *discussed* in a specific and scheduled follow-up session, express your appreciation and be certain that the feedback recipient perceives your sincerity in saying "Thank you."

Your expression of genuine appreciation for the employee or colleague's willingness to join you in a feedback discussion will go a long way toward establishing—and above all *reinforcing*—a relationship that will transform a willingness to join a feedback session into an enthusiasm for those sessions—and above all for the positive results they produce. A crucial part of achieving those goals comes at the end of the session when, confident that your feedback message has been received, and is understood, you set the stage for the next step.

NINE

Feedback in Special or Difficult Situations

Providing valid, worthwhile feedback requires candor and avoids rose-colored glasses.

The same is true for a book about feedback. So let's be candid: not every feedback situation will proceed without incident. More to the point, not every situation you encounter as a manager, supervisor or colleague can be addressed by feedback alone. For some situations and circumstances a feedback approach, even a revolutionary one, may be inappropriate.

Let's look at some of the most common special or difficult feedback situations, and the best ways to address them.

FAILURE TO IMPROVE: SERIOUS PERFORMANCE PROBLEMS

As you know, my definition of feedback is that it's information shared for the distinct purpose of improving results or relationships.

Note that key word: *improving.*

You undertake a feedback journey with an employee because you are confident that the employee is capable of improved performance and will embrace the improvement plan you develop together.

Occasionally, though, an employee will fail to meet the improvement targets. Because your feedback plan included specific goals and schedules for improvement, you should become aware of the problem before it becomes a major issue. Your next steps will be pure revolutionary feedback:

- **Meet with the employee and discuss the issues.**
  Determine if there are factors—including external factors—that may be causing the failure to improve.

- **Listen attentively to the employee's explanation for the difficulty.** Respond appropriately.

- **Re-work the schedule of improvement targets, making clear that any additional resources are available.**

- **Make clear the seriousness of the situation**—and do so in a positive fashion, reinforcing your confidence that the employee can and *will* turn things around.

If the employee continues to miss goals and fails to improve, your next steps will be determined by the structure of your company or organization, but could include:

- **Discussion of whether the employee is in the wrong job.**

  - Meet with your peers to discuss possibility or appropriateness of transferring the employee to another department.

- **Formal probationary period**—Human Resources may need to sign off on this—to provide the employee with another, final chance to accomplish the improvement goals needed to maintain her or his employment. Make clear that this is a very serious step.

- It should be made clear to the employee that this is the penultimate stage in the process; failure here will result in:

- **Termination.**

Termination of an employee is a special situation and is never pleasant. Your feedback skills still play an important role in this process.

TERMINATION

When terminating an employee for performance-related reasons, you should maintain your positive tone—as much as possible. Just as important, the effect the action will have on the employee's life and family. Communicate that awareness subtly, offering your confidence that the employee will find a more suitable position. It is wise to consult with your Human Resources Department what conversation points you are and are not permitted to say in this situation. Be aware that your words are likely to be unwelcomed and that you do not owe an apology. Practice empathy—you know that the employee's life will be disrupted by the loss of employment.

And also be aware of the multiple steps you and your company have taken to turn around the employee's performance. Don't blame or shame the employee; this has no more a place in a termination than in any other aspect of the feedback process. Do make clear your sincere regret that things didn't work out.

In the case of termination for behavioral or legal reasons—not performance reasons, your posture will be different, more formal. In all likelihood the termination will involve the presence of Human Resources and, possibly, legal or security personnel. In such circumstances feedback may be not only inappropriate, also irrelevant. You say no more than is necessary, and you should present your comments as objectively as possible.

LAYOFFS AND REDUCTIONS IN FORCE

When employees are let go for business reasons, and not performance or behavioral reasons, your feedback skills will be challenged—and needed. If you've ever been in the position of being let go for reasons beyond your control, and despite excellent performance of your job, you have a good idea of what your employees are going through.

In such circumstances, your ability to remain within your Feedback Zone will be challenged and will also play a large part in helping you and your employees through a difficult professional situation.

Layoffs and reductions in force are coordinated with the Human Resources Department, which will provide you with guidance and counsel regarding what you are allowed to say, and how the termination information will be presented. Armed with that expert input, your feedback skills should be put to work ensuring that you:

- **Make clear that the loss of employment is a result of business conditions, and has nothing to do with the employee's performance or the importance of her or his contribution to the company.**

- **Communicate your appreciation for the effort the employees made; if appropriate, let them know that you have enjoyed working with them.**

- **Express your confidence that the employee will land on her or his feet, and that the next employer will be lucky to have her or him.**

- **Discuss the resources—severance pay, outplacement services, etc.—that the company will be offering.**

- **Allow them, within reason, to vent their concerns.**

- **Offer, if permitted by your company, and if appropriate for specific employees, any assistance you can personally offer as they seek new employment.**

None of this will be easy, but your employees and co-workers will appreciate it, whether or not that appreciation is evident (probably not!)—at the time.

EXIT INTERVIEWS: FEEDBACK AND FAREWELL

Sometimes high-performing employees who make important and valuable contributions to your company move on. There are almost as many causes for this as there are employees. Some include:

- **Change of career.**

- **Relocation for family or other personal reasons.**

- **Income or appealing job offer.**

Whatever the reason, your exit interview with the departing employee provides an opportunity to use your feedback skills in a different manner, discussing with the employees their experience with your company, and the ways in which that experience affected their decision to leave (if it did).

To begin, seek advice from Human Resources regarding:

- **Proprietary information the employee possesses, and how to make clear that the information cannot be shared.**

- **Non-compete clauses, if applicable, that would make the new employer, possibly a competitor, off-limits.**

- **What materials and items the employee is permitted to take with her or him.**

- **How long the employee is—or is not—expected to remain on the job before departure.**

Ideally, the exit interview will be a pleasant, if perhaps wistful, feedback conversation on both sides of the table. You will naturally be curious about whether or not anything could have been done differently to retain the employee. Such questions should be posed subtly, unless you are making a counter-offer.

Above all, you will be using your feedback skills to get a final sense of the departing employee's impressions of both the company and work experience there, and also her or his experience of working with you as manager, supervisor or colleague. Encourage candor, and accept the comments and insights with good grace, even (and maybe especially) if you don't agree. With some luck and some help from a healthy workplace culture, exit interviews will be rare and the feedback you receive will be positive and informative.

TEN

Your Feedback Revolution=Your Feedback Culture

Feedback revolutions are deliberate, contagious and beneficial to all. In closing I want to talk with you about the larger and ongoing contributions your *feedback revolution* will make to your company as a whole and its processes and culture.

Effective feedback is specific and carefully crafted. For feedback to work, your message must be *delivered* on a personal level, not a standardized one.

Feedback revolutions don't take place in a vacuum. Successful feedback revolutions spread outward from the first time you make the approach your own and make effective feedback practices central to your communications. As this becomes part of your daily routine, you have ignited your revolution. Every step of the feedback process sends signals that the culture of your organization is changing, becoming more open and innovative. The simple ingredients of effective feedback—specific, timely, positive—draw a vibrant contrast to the starkness of traditional performance evaluations and their armature.

At the risk of violating my rule about maintaining a positive stance (for informational purposes!), let's review what an annual performance review communicates (regardless of the nature of the content):

- **Fixed and rigid evaluation categories: general rather than specific**

- **Reduction of employee performance—and by extension employee worth—to a set of static numbers and impersonal checkboxes**

- **Infrequent, and thus rarely (if ever) timely**

- **Monologue rather than conversation**

- **Perfunctory rather than positive**

- **Required participation: no permission requests**

- **Rarely includes appreciation or gratitude**

The message sent by this approach is one with which we are all-too familiar. Performance reviews—and other mandated management and supervisory communications—can seem remote, monolithic, impersonal, and faceless.

Real feedback, I remind you, is different.

Real, genuine feedback at the level I've described in this book is a *human* process, natural and supple rather than artificial, static or rigid. The fundamental tenets of this approach to creating a **feedback revolution** are solidly thought-through and proven in practice. They're also designed to provide you with the maximum flexibility that you, as any manager or supervisor, need in order to deal with the variety of situations and circumstances that your career and profession throw at you.

In other words, this isn't about adopting the model of "Margie Mauldin's Feedback Revolution" and putting it in place—without a set of checkboxes or numbered steps, one hopes—in your company.

Far from it! My goal with this book, and with the *iLoveFeedback*® program, is to provide you with a set of tools that, as you master them, can be tailored to your unique management style and goals—and shaped by all of those other factors that have contributed to making you, *you*!

Like any valuable set of tools, there are certain fundamentals that will guide their application. Your increasing familiarity with these tools will allow you to make adjustments and adaptations, putting your own "spin" on things, making them *your own*...a human process.

As you begin to see the results that the *feedback revolution* produces in your workplace, look for the positive effects to accelerate and spread, and rejoice in your *feedback revolution*.

As your employees and co-workers become more and more aware of the changes you've instituted and of the results—measurable in terms of both productivity and environmental, as well as morale and enthusiasm—you may well find them asking how you've gone about accomplishing the transformation. They may begin to adopt and adapt the principles and techniques of the *feedback revolution* to their own jobs and teams. Be prepared to have co-workers and employees come directly to you to learn more about effective feedback. You will find that you are ready to help them, armed with the variety of tips, tools and tactics that encourage and nurture ongoing feedback success. And be ready to have them come to you with feedback of their own! That's a sure sign that the *feedback revolution* is taking off, and you are in the process of creating—alongside your colleagues, co-workers and employees—a *Feedback Culture* in your workplace. Once established, such a culture becomes self-reinforcing and self-nourishing. Everyone wants to do better, to improve—and the ***feedback revolution*** shows them that they can.

Your own personal improvement path will benefit as well. The procedures and practices that enable great feedback are the foundation upon which your *Feedback Culture* stands. The day-to-day practice of feedback will be malleable and adaptable, with different situations and challenges calling upon different levels and arrays of feedback skills in order to achieve the optimum result. All of this driven by the definition that is the heart of the ***feedback revolution***, and the heart of your *Feedback Culture*:

Good luck with your ***feedback revolution!*** I look forward to hearing all about it, and about the ways you've put the lessons of this book to work and made them your own.

So get in touch—my contact information is at the back of the book.

Don't be shy. As you may have gathered:

I Love Feedback!

"I'll have someone from my generation get in touch with someone from your generation."

Feedback Across the Generations

Do you find as much grievance as guffaw in this cartoon?

You're not alone.

Differences among the generations are nothing new. They weren't new in the 1960s when the term "Generation Gap" became common. They also weren't new, for that matter, in Shakespeare's time either—or even earlier.

Prowl among the artifacts of the earliest civilizations, the bits and scraps of writing that have survived from the dawn of civilization, and you'll come across ancient wisdom along the lines of: *Things aren't what they used to be. The new generation doesn't—*

You get the picture.

Differences among the generations, and the communications challenges those differences pose, are as old as our species. What is new about the times we live in is the *number of generations working side-by-side.* While at one time it was common for multi-generational families to work a farm, or for one generation to follow another into the same factory, what's happened over the past few decades is different. People are living longer and working longer. As a result, it's not unusual to find four generations in one work environment today.

The opportunities and benefits of this situation are huge—yet they are opportunities and benefits that are rarely harvested, and often ignored because of that age-old "generation gap" and the communications complications it carries. The real problem is a *communication* gap, not necessarily a generational gap. Either way it's still a gap—one that ideas, innovations, improvements, and insights fall into and are never heard from again.

What to do about it?

Put in place a new approach to feedback—a **Feedback Revolution!**—that acknowledges, adjusts for, and above all celebrates the resources and perspectives that different generations bring to the workplace.

WHOSE GENERATION GAP? SHAKESPEARE REVISITED

I'll bet that by the time you finish this appendix—and maybe even before—you'll see that effective feedback, by its very nature, works with *every* generation. You just have to tailor its presentation and delivery to match the recipient. But, as the previous chapters showed, you would be doing that anyway, whether the recipient is 20 years older than you, 20 years younger, or born on the same date in the same year as you.

At the same time, there are some *general* generational differences to keep in mind; understanding these differences and using that understanding to guide your feedback will go a long way toward ensuring that your message isn't swallowed by the generation gap. And there's one specific difference in today's workplace, a difference that makes it vital for managers to develop their cross-generational understanding. The difference? Simple:

For the first time, it's becoming common to have four and, in some cases, five generations represented among the workers in a single company.

This is new, and it's a situation that presents enormous opportunities as well as challenges.

Two, and often three, generations working a family farm was once the norm. Likewise, many industries used to see several generations of workers pass through their gates—the younger apprenticed to the older, following in their parents' footsteps. In an era where many, if not most, occupations including professions and skilled labor involved an apprenticeship, generations working alongside each other was common—and, more importantly, *structured*. The younger worker was apprenticed to an older one for a period of time during which the experience, knowledge, and skill involved in the job was passed from the senior generation to the junior.

Here is the stuff of our history, and of a surprising number of novels and movies. This is the *big* difference between the old days and the present...between *then* and *now*. Things are different today. While many businesses and organizations do institute mentoring programs for younger team members, that process differs in many ways from the cross-generational training that apprenticeship provided.

In terms of feedback, many young workers are thrown directly into the workforce at higher than entry-level positions. For the "best and the brightest," the "Whiz Kids," or whatever the cream of each year's crop from our most prestigious universities and advanced degree programs is called, those positions—and salaries—can be *far* higher than traditional entry-level posts.

Today's multi-generational workforce is not a consequence of family ownership (although that can still apply in certain cases), nor is it a product of proximity to the local factory. Rather, the spread of ages in a company today is the result of factors that have been building for the last half-century:

- **People are living longer, and are thus working longer— whether by choice or necessity.**

- **People are remaining vigorously engaged with their work longer.**

- **The youngest generations entering the workplace are doing so with skills—and outlooks—shaped not only by previous generations including their parents, also by an educational, social, and technological landscape that is radically different from what preceded it.**

Additionally, as a result of the technological advances and upheavals of the last couple of decades, the organizational structure—particularly the relationship among the generations within that structure—has been altered.

The "Whiz Kid Effect"—think Bill Gates and Steve Jobs a quarter-century ago, Mark Zuckerberg more recently, and many others of varying levels of spectacular success (or failure in between)—has seen some *very* young people running very large companies, while managing much older employees.

This too is different. While long shelves of novels and movies offer windows into how previous eras handled the cross-generational challenge, that handling generally fell into a fairly narrow range:

- **"Old Bull" Versus "Young Bull"**

- **Wise Elder Teaches Young Whippersnapper a Lesson or Two**

- **Young Whippersnapper Teaches Wise Elder a Lesson or Two**

- **Elder and Whippersnapper Never Do Learn Anything and Destroy the Company in the Process**

There are other variations—Young Whippersnapper Marries Wise Elder's Child (which was Wise Elder's plan all along)—but these are the basics.

What they have in common was that for all the drama—or comedy—in the telling, they reaffirmed a "natural order of things"; young people growing into the roles formerly held by their elders. In other words:

To everything, there is a season . . .

One famous approach to the passing of time can be found in Shakespeare's *As You Like It*, which has reminded us since the 1600s that as we move through the ages of life, we also move through different roles—from youthful exuberance (and joyful foolhardiness!) to elderly wisdom (and infirmity). You may remember the passage—but in case you don't, I've included it below. The passage is as poignant and relevant today as it was more than four centuries ago.

As the Bard Said...

All the world's a stage,
And all the men and women merely players:
They have their exits and their entrances;
And one man in his time plays many parts,
His acts being seven ages. At first, the infant,
Mewling and puking in the nurse's arms.
And then the whining school-boy, with his satchel
And shining morning face, creeping like snail
Unwillingly to school. And then the lover,
Sighing like furnace, with a woeful ballad
Made to his mistress' eyebrow. Then a soldier,
Full of strange oaths and bearded like the pard,
Jealous in honour, sudden and quick in quarrel,
Seeking the bubble reputation
Even in the cannon's mouth. And then the justice,
In fair round belly with good capon lined,
With eyes severe and beard of formal cut,
Full of wise saws and modern instances;
And so he plays his part. The sixth age shifts
Into the lean and slipper'd pantaloon,
With spectacles on nose and pouch on side,
His youthful hose, well saved, a world too wide
For his shrunk shank; and his big manly voice,
Turning again toward childish treble, pipes
And whistles in his sound. Last scene of all,
That ends this strange eventful history,
Is second childishness and mere oblivion,
Sans teeth, sans eyes, sans taste, sans everything.

—William Shakespeare, *As You Like It*

Now, clearly you won't be working with the first or second of Shakespeare's Ages—if you have infant or child employees, you've got larger labor law challenges than feedback can resolve!—and likely not with the seventh. But all those "stages" in between may be represented in your workforce, perhaps even on a single team. Shakespeare's catalog has some useful reminders for dealing with each of them.

But these aren't Shakespeare's times. These aren't even Neil Simon's times anymore!

It's no surprise to anyone whose eyes and ears are open that the "natural order" has been turned upside down, pulled inside out, and twisted sideways by societal changes. *Every* generation is working next to every other generation now, and *that's* the *new* natural order of things.

In this multi-generational workforce, a manager must know how to reach each age group with effective feedback. As I've shown throughout this book, crafting effective feedback has as much to do with your sense of the person you're providing feedback to as it does with the content of the feedback itself. Let's make that even clearer:

- *Effective feedback seamlessly combines content—the feedback message—with your understanding of the person receiving the feedback.*

- *The two are mutually reinforcing, and, ultimately inextricable.*

If you approach the modern, multi-generational workforce with these thoughts in mind . . .

You will be able to tailor your feedback both to the employee's particular needs and *to that employee's generational expectations.*

The Generations

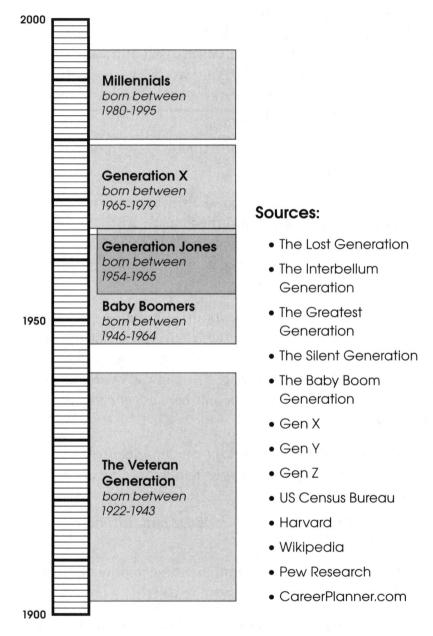

2000

Millennials
*born between
1980-1995*

Generation X
*born between
1965-1979*

Generation Jones
*born between
1954-1965*

Baby Boomers
*born between
1946-1964*

1950

**The Veteran
Generation**
*born between
1922-1943*

1900

Sources:

- The Lost Generation
- The Interbellum Generation
- The Greatest Generation
- The Silent Generation
- The Baby Boom Generation
- Gen X
- Gen Y
- Gen Z
- US Census Bureau
- Harvard
- Wikipedia
- Pew Research
- CareerPlanner.com

Generation dates are approximate and may overlap. There are no fixed, standard years for when a generation begins and ends. This chart is provided as a reference guide for *Appendix A*.

FEEDBACK REVOLUTION

Here are some **TIPS, TOOLS, & TACTICS** to help you navigate the giving and receiving of feedback across the generations.

TIPS, TOOLS, & TACTICS: *MILLENNIALS*

TIPS

- Be specific, as with all feedback. Get to the point quickly.

- Use Millennials' impatience to your advantage—set up goals and deliverables that can be achieved quickly (set up incremental or staged goals if necessary).

- Conversely, use your feedback sessions to begin to show Millennials that in some cases, slower and steadier wins races.

TOOLS

- Use Millennial's technology comfort levels to your advantage—and to the advantage of your feedback! Email, text messages, video chats, and PowerPoint presentations can be effective feedback tools with Millennials.

- Get to your point quickly, using only as much time as needed.

TACTICS

- Make lists and summaries of feedback—and have the Millennial employee do the same. Then compare lists!

- Don't forget to add humor—and, if appropriate, irony—to your feedback sessions.

TIPS, TOOLS, & TACTICS: *GENERATION X*

TIPS

- Generation X loves challenges: Make sure not only that their work includes stimulating projects and thought-provoking responsibilities, also that your feedback includes new challenging opportunities.

- Find areas where flexibility and nonstandard approaches to tasks and responsibilities can be introduced or implemented.

- Treat the other person with respect and allow her or him to be an active participant in the discussion.

TOOLS

- Use technology to enhance and extend feedback sessions.

- Think about providing a printed copy of their evaluation, something tangible they can take home.

- Don't be shy about offering them further training if you feel—or more importantly if *they* feel—that their potential is not fully being tapped.

TACTICS

- Limit feedback-related paperwork as much as possible.

- Get to the point quickly and clearly, focusing as much energy on the consequences and ongoing opportunities that result from the feedback as on the feedback itself.

- Bear in mind that Generation X employees are likely to be resistant to responsibilities that limit their time with family—negotiate the balance that best suits your employee's family concerns as well as your business goals.

- Offer direction balanced with plenty of freedom and flexibility for them to complete the project their way, incorporating their creativity and innovation.

- Reward positive performance swiftly—don't wait.

TIPS, TOOLS, & TACTICS: *GENERATION JONES*
(LATE BABY BOOMERS TO EARLY GEN-XERS)

TIPS

- Generation Jones employees have reached the stage of their careers where they are willing—and determined—to be discerning. Be prepared for pushback or negotiation when offering new responsibilities or increased workload.

- Idealism and cynicism coexist in Generation Jones— address this duality in your feedback.

- Generation Jones is accustomed to having plenty of choices and options—structure your feedback sessions, if possible, in such a way as to offer choices, options, menus of possibilities.

TOOLS

- Incentives are important to this generation—tailor your feedback to include appealing incentives when appropriate or deserved.

- There can be more—much more—to an incentive or reward system than financial compensation. In feedback sessions, discuss the sorts of incentives or rewards that the specific employee most desires or prefers. Perhaps a flexible schedule would be worth more than a dollar-figure raise.

- Don't get carried away with technology—Generation Jones appreciates the benefits of new technologies but maintains a solid perspective that keeps technology "in its proper place."

TACTICS

- Bring big questions to the feedback session: Long-term goals, security, and late-stage career growth are all on Generation Jones' mind and should play a part in the feedback session.

- Generation Jones is also at the point where career transition may be under consideration—discuss ways in which the employee and your business can mutually benefit from such transitions, if the employee desires a change.

TIPS, TOOLS, & TACTICS: *BABY BOOMERS*

TIPS

- Boomers are an extraordinarily diverse group. As with all other generations, don't lump all your boomer employees into a single cluster.

- Boomers are willing and even eager to experiment, and their age and work experience make it likely that their experiments will be both innovative and practical—tailor your feedback to invite their creativity.

- Big goals are vitally important to boomers, who are eager to make sure that they have "made their mark"—your feedback sessions should be aimed at determining what the employee's large, as well as near- and short-term, goals should be.

TOOLS

- Despite boomers' comfort levels with technology, some may prefer to have paper copies of feedback materials as well as digital ones.

TACTICS

- Retirement—or, in challenging economic times, financial security—is beginning to be much on the boomers' minds; feedback sessions should include acknowledgment of big picture planning and strategizing as well as short- or near-term goals.

- Boomers have reached the point in their lives where family responsibilities and obligations are changing, often in dramatic ways. Tuition and other expenses associated with college-aged children along with caring for aging parents are topics that may affect boomers' goals, and these should be discussed honestly and tactfully in feedback sessions.

- Give the employee the floor and listen to what she or he has to say—boomers have both opinions and the experience to back up their opinions, and their comments during feedback sessions can be invaluable for both the employee and your business.

TIPS, TOOLS, & TACTICS:
THE VETERAN GENERATION

TIPS

- Be aware that 65+ feedback recipients are aware that they are in the latter stages of their careers.

- While I'm frequently amazed at how physically vigorous many people past 65 are, and how insightful their thoughts are, I'm also aware that this isn't true of everyone. People past 65 simply do not have the endless supply of physical energy they possessed when younger—no matter how much they think they do.

- Don't raise your voice or simplify your language because of the feedback recipient's age—don't condescend.

TOOLS

- Many over-sixty-fivers are uncomfortable or even wary and anxious about new technologies; as with boomers, consider teaming them with younger, more tech-savvy employees to the benefit of both.

TACTICS

- Over-sixty-five employees are chronologically in the latter stages of their careers; your awareness of this, handled gracefully and tactfully in your feedback, will help ease any concerns they fear about being "put out to pasture."

- Should an over-sixty-five employee's age begin to affect her or his ability to perform a job or fulfill responsibilities, your feedback should be honest and at the same time delicate— can you find another function the employee can fulfill? The challenge is to maintain the employee's self-respect—and value to the company—without jeopardizing the business or, far more importantly, the employee's safety and health.

WHAT GENERATION GAP?

The best way to bridge—or eliminate—generation gaps, whether real or perceived, is to bring the generations together as much as possible, depending upon the generational composition of your team. Take liberties to shape the team to be sure it embraces different styles of thinking as well as different ages. Cross-generational teams are almost *de facto* **Feedback Factories;** regularly maintained and encouraged, they will become genuine, authentic **Feedback Factories** in no time. Here are a couple of examples of feedback that flow easily through cross-generational teams.

- Older-generational members can show the younger ones the "ropes"—their experience becomes a living thing in cross-generational teams.

- Younger members who are more comfortable with technology can show the older-generational teammates how to use some of the new tools and, if your team structure permits, take some of the technology-related responsibilities off the older-generational members' hands. This can alleviate any potential pressure older-generational employees may feel if confronted with new digital tools.

Remember:

A Feedback Culture

    Equals

Generation Feedback

Which

    Generates

Great Feedback!

Feedback and Technology

As I've made clear throughout the book, feedback is most effective when delivered personally, with both giver and recipient present. Because conversation is so central to effective feedback, I highly recommend that every effort be made to arrange personal presence for important feedback sessions. If mutual physical presence isn't possible—due to remote offices or installations, for example—telephone and video-conferences can be used.

Other technologies—and sometimes it seems as if there's a new one every day—can be used to reinforce feedback, provide check-ins and updates, but only rarely should they be used as substitutes or surrogates for a full face-to-face feedback session.

That said, we must also acknowledge that we live and work in a technology-driven world, with communications-based technology the prime driver. It would be foolish to avoid the use of these technologies—and ones not yet developed—as part of our *feedback revolution.* Here are a few brief comments on the possible roles of modern and innovative communications technologies in your *feedback revolution.* I'll address the two primary technologies likely to be of best service to your *feedback revolution:* Email and Txts.

YOU'VE GOT FEEDBACK

How good a medium for *feedback* is email?

Depends on the type of feedback you're sending. For follow-up and follow-through messages, building upon a foundation established in a person-to-person feedback session, email can be quite effective, offering a variety of benefits and advantages. Email is:

- **Fast**

- **Available on multiple platforms**

- **Automatically date- and time-stamped**

- **A more permanent record than a phone call**

- **A "trail" of commentary and response**

Bearing these virtues in mind, let's look at the deficits of email:

- **Relatively impersonal and completely faceless**

- **High potential to be hasty and imprecise when "dashing off" an email**

- **Easy to mis-address or mis-send an email**

Of these, it is the bland impersonality of email that should directly affect your choice of email as a feedback medium. It would be wise to restrict, or even eliminate, email as a *primary* medium for feedback.

After all:

Effective business feedback is never faceless.

CAN U TXT FDBK?

The easy answer is:

NO U CANT!

But, used judiciously, txts can offer excellent opportunities to reinforce and reinvigorate feedback given in more substantial conversations. Keeping in mind that txts are not appropriate—or even capable because of length limitations—for detailed feedback, they *can* be effective tools for:

- **Concise statements of information relevant to feedback**

- **Acknowledgments and confirmations**

- **Changes in schedule and other agenda items**

- **Quick bursts of enthusiasm and encouragement**

- **Brief updates and follow-throughs**

Txts are *not* good for:

- **Substantive or nuanced information**

- **Negative information or feedback**

- **Detailed analyses or reviews**

SOCIAL MEDIA IS NO PLACE FOR PROFESSIONAL FEEDBACK

Feedback is a *personal* conversation between you and an employee or colleague. Just as the contents of your feedback sessions should not be shared with others in the organization, neither should your feedback show up on Facebook, Twitter, Instagram, Tumblr, Snapchat nor any other trending social media platform of the time. Social media may have useful and dynamic qualities, but providing a platform for employee feedback is definitely NOT one of them.

Technology is a tool, and knowing which tools are appropriate for aspects of your *feedback revolution,* and more importantly which are not, is a skill that will become more and more important as the technological revolution continues to gain speed.

TIPS, TOOLS, & TACTICS

TIPS:

- If possible, respond in kind to electronic messages—a txt to you should receive a txt in return (if it requires any reply at all), an email an email, and so on. (And by the way, I feel the same way about wine; Italian wine with the foods of Italy, French with the French, California wine with American food, and so forth.)

  - When your reply to a txt would require more space than a txt permits, for instance, say so in a txt:

    Ths needs mre discussion—call me @ 2pm

- Use appropriate language, salutation, and other conventions for various technologies:

  - Abbreviations acceptable in a txt are not acceptable in an email, for instance.

  - Review the rules with all direct reports and team members.

- When a direct report comes up with an especially effective approach to using technology in the course of work, share the approach with the rest of the team. Discuss and analyze what makes it effective, and look for ways to adapt the approach to other purposes—and possibly other technologies.

TOOLS:

- Consider designing an email form for your direct reports (and other members of your team), essentially an electronic letterhead that identifies your direct reports as part of your group—this may require checking with your overall company policy, and, if approved, having the form designed.

- If the members of your team use their own technology—BYOD (Bring Your Own Device) is catching on at many companies—make sure that all communications between your device (including software) and theirs can be opened and read.

- Paper still has a place—an important one! Put to use the definite advantages of paper media, including:
  - Stationery
  - Greeting cards
  - Post cards
  - Printed newsletters (but only if they've got something to say!)

TACTICS:

- Instruct your direct reports never to send internal emails from unsecured public Internet access points and hotspots.

- Standardize security measures and procedures among your direct reports, ensuring that all are up-to-date on virus protection, frequency of changing passwords, and understanding how to avoid exposing themselves—and your feedback—to unwanted intrusions.

- Put together a team-wide newsletter (whether on paper or electronically) focused on general feedback about your business. Invite—or demand, if necessary—regular participation from all members.

- Find out who among your direct reports is most tech-savvy, then use her or him as a resource for all members of your team.

The *iLoveFeedback*® Program

Feedback—timely, specific, two-way feedback is among the most effective communications tools we possess. And while we all possess the ability to master the art of giving effective feedback, most of us have not developed the skills necessary to do so. And we lack the skills because most of us don't actually know what the elements of effective feedback are.

The *iLoveFeedback*® training program was created to remedy that situation, and to remedy in an enjoyable, inviting and above all, practical way. The program was created to give you the tools you will need to create a ***feedback revolution*** in your organization. The program's purpose is to clear away the fog and misunderstandings that surround feedback as typically practiced and replace them with clarity, tools, and techniques for putting real feedback in place in your organization.

iLoveFeedback® is a dynamic half-day workshop that provides individuals with the skills and confidence for providing effective feedback. The program outlines the 5 Best Practice Steps for feedback with clearly-defined learning objectives, real-life application exercises, practical tools to reinforce skills, and tips for successful implementation. *iLoveFeedback*® can also be successfully delivered from a virtual platform.

iLoveFeedback® rests upon experience, observation and research—every tip, tool or tactic presented has been tested in business and has demonstrated consistent effectiveness in the real world.

About Executive Forum

Executive Forum is a leadership training and development company founded in 1986. We apply our expertise to help clients define success and develop a customized approach to achieve it consistently. We do this by introducing new tools through our Leadership Series®, transferring skills through award-winning training programs, and implementing a proven process for realizing repeatable success through our tailored services. It's an established approach that benefits the organization by empowering individuals with enhanced skills and confidence.

Other programs by Executive Forum

A speaker series created to strengthen professional leadership skills such as communication, innovation, team-building and strategic planning.

An eLearning platform designed to deliver innovative leadership development content using a blended learning approach of documents, audio/video files and facilitator guides.